Ronda Travel Guide 2024

A Simple and Comprehensive Guidebook on Everything You Need to Know About Visiting Unveiling Ronda (Soul of Andalusia), Spain.

Alfredo Martin

Table of Contents

Introduction to Ronda   1

  Unveiling Andalusia's Timeless Charm   1

  A Glimpse into Ronda's Rich History   1

  Discovering Ronda's Geographical Wonders   3

  Understanding Ronda's Cultural Heritage   5

Chapter 1   9

Getting Acquainted with Ronda   9

  Navigating Ronda's Charming Streets and Alleys   9

  Exploring Ronda's Iconic Landmarks   11

  Sampling Ronda's Gastronomic Delights   14

Chapter 2   17

Immersing in Ronda's Culture   17

  Flamenco: The Heartbeat of Ronda   17

  Festivals and Celebrations: Embracing Ronda's Vibrant Spirit   19

  Art and Architecture   22

Chapter 3   27

Outdoor Nature Escapes in Ronda   27

  Hiking the Trails   27

  Exploring the Surrounding Countryside   29

Tajo de Ronda: Admiring Nature's Sculpture   31

Chapter 4   35

Ronda's Hidden Gems   35

Secret Gardens and Scenic Views   35

Off the Beaten Path: The Thrill of Discovery   37

Wine Tasting in Ronda: A Toast to Tradition   38

Chapter 5   41

Practical Tips for Travelers   41

Getting Around Ronda: Transportation Tips and Tricks   41

Accommodation Options for Every Budget   43

Essential Phrases and Local Etiquette   45

Chapter 6   49

Beyond Ronda: Day Trips and Excursions   49

Coastal Escapes   51

Day Trips to Nearby Cultural Gems   53

Chapter 7   57

Ronda: A Photographer's Paradise   57

Capturing Ronda's Essence Through the Lens   57

Photography Tips and Spots   60

Conclusion: Farewell to Ronda   63

Reflecting on Ronda's Timeless Allure   63

Introduction to Ronda

Unveiling Andalusia's Timeless Charm

Nestled amidst the breathtaking landscapes of Andalusia, Ronda emerges as a captivating jewel, weaving together a tapestry of rich history, geographical wonders, and vibrant cultural heritage. As you embark on your journey through Ronda, prepare to be enchanted by its timeless allure and profound significance in Spanish history and culture.

A Glimpse into Ronda's Rich History

To truly appreciate Ronda's allure, one must delve into its storied past, which dates back thousands of years. Ronda stands as a testament to the enduring legacies of civilizations that once flourished in this region. From its ancient origins as a Moorish stronghold to its pivotal role in the Spanish Conquistador, Ronda's history is a captivating narrative of conquests, conflicts, and cultural exchanges.

Take a stroll through the cobbled streets of Ronda's Old Town, where echoes of the past resonate in every corner. Explore the imposing walls of the Alcazaba, a Moorish fortress that offers panoramic views of the surrounding countryside. Marvel at the intricate architecture of the Palacio de Mondragón, a palatial residence that reflects Ronda's Moorish and Renaissance influences.

As you wander through Ronda's labyrinthine alleys, immerse yourself in the stories of its illustrious inhabitants, from legendary bandits to celebrated poets. Visit the Museo Lara, a cultural institution housed in a meticulously restored 18thcentury mansion, where artifacts and exhibits unravel the mysteries of Ronda's past.

To enrich your understanding of Ronda's history, consider joining a guided tour led by knowledgeable locals or historians. These tours offer invaluable insights into Ronda's historical landmarks, providing context and depth to your exploration. Prices for guided tours typically range from $20 to $50 per person, depending on the duration and inclusions.

Opening Times:

Alcazaba: Open daily from 10:00 AM to 6:00 PM

Palacio de Mondragón: Open Tuesday to Sunday from 10:00 AM to 5:00 PM

Museo Lara: Open daily from 10:00 AM to 7:00 PM

Discovering Ronda's Geographical Wonders

Ronda's geographical landscape is a testament to

nature's aweinspiring grandeur, characterized by dramatic cliffs, rugged mountains, and the majestic Guadalevín River gorge. The crown jewel of Ronda's natural wonders is undoubtedly the Puente Nuevo, an iconic bridge that spans the depths of El Tajo gorge, connecting the old and new quarters of the city.

To behold the breathtaking vistas of Ronda's landscape, embark on a leisurely stroll along the Paseo de Blas Infante, a scenic promenade that offers panoramic views of the surrounding countryside. Admire the cascading waterfalls of the Cueva del Gato, a hidden gem nestled amidst lush vegetation and limestone formations.

For the adventurous at heart, hiking trails such as the Camino de los Molinos and the Sendero de los Alcornocales offer immersive experiences amidst nature's splendor. Traverse rugged terrain, traverse forests, and encounter hidden waterfalls as you explore the pristine wilderness surrounding Ronda.

To capture the essence of Ronda's geographical wonders, consider embarking on a guided hiking excursion led by experienced local guides. These excursions typically range from $30 to $80 per person, depending on the duration and difficulty level.

Opening Times:

Paseo de Blas Infante: Open daily, accessible throughout the day

Cueva del Gato: Accessible year round, best visited during daylight hours

Hiking Trails: Open year round, with varying degrees of difficulty and accessibility

Understanding Ronda's Cultural Heritage

Ronda's cultural heritage is a vibrant tapestry woven

from centuries of artistic expression, culinary traditions, and festive celebrations. At the heart of Ronda's cultural identity lies its deeprooted connections to flamenco, a passionate art form that embodies the soul of Andalusia.

Immerse yourself in the rhythms and melodies of flamenco by attending a live performance at one of Ronda's renowned tablaos or flamenco venues. Experience the raw emotion and virtuosity of flamenco dancers, accompanied by the soulful strains of guitar and vocals. Prices for flamenco performances range from $20 to $50 per person, depending on the venue and seating options.

Throughout the year, Ronda comes alive with vibrant festivals and celebrations that pay homage to its cultural heritage. Experience the exhilarating atmosphere of the Feria de Pedro Romero, a weeklong fiesta that commemorates Ronda's bullfighting tradition. Witness colorful parades, traditional music, and exhilarating bullfights that capture the essence of Andalusian culture.

For a taste of Ronda's culinary delights, embark on a gastronomic journey through its bustling markets and quaint tapas bars. Indulge in savory delicacies such as jamón ibérico, salmorejo, and traditional Andalusian gazpacho, accompanied by fine wines from the region's renowned vineyards.

To deepen your understanding of Ronda's cultural heritage, consider participating in handson workshops and culinary experiences led by local artisans and chefs. Learn the art of traditional Spanish cooking, explore the intricacies of flamenco dance, or unleash your creativity through pottery and painting classes.

Opening Times:

Flamenco Performances: Scheduled evenings, typically starting from 8:00 PM onwards

Feria de Pedro Romero: Held annually in September, with festivities lasting throughout the week

Tapas Bars and Markets: Open daily, with varying hours of operation

As you embark on your journey through Ronda, let its rich history, geographical wonders, and cultural heritage captivate your senses and ignite your spirit of adventure. Prepare to be swept away by the timeless charm of this enchanting Andalusian gem, where every cobblestone tells a story, and every moment is a celebration of life.

Chapter 1

Getting Acquainted with Ronda

Embracing the Essence of Andalusia

In the heart of Andalusia lies the captivating city of Ronda, where every cobblestone street and ancient alleyway beckons travelers to explore its rich tapestry of history, culture, and gastronomy. As you embark on your journey to discover Ronda's treasures, immerse yourself in the essence of Andalusian charm and hospitality.

Navigating Ronda's Charming Streets and Alleys

Step into a world where time seems to stand still as you meander through Ronda's charming streets and alleys. Begin your exploration in the heart of the city, Plaza del

Socorro, where the pulse of Ronda beats to the rhythm of daily life. From here, let your curiosity be your guide as you wander through narrow cobblestone lanes adorned with whitewashed facades and vibrant bougainvillea.

Take a leisurely stroll along Calle La Bola, a picturesque thoroughfare lined with quaint cafes, artisan shops, and hidden courtyards. Lose yourself in the labyrinthine alleys of Ronda's Old Town, where every twist and turn reveals a new discovery waiting to be made.

To truly immerse yourself in the local ambiance, consider joining a guided walking tour led by knowledgeable locals. These tours offer invaluable insights into Ronda's history, architecture, and culture, providing a deeper appreciation for the city's storied past. Prices for guided walking tours typically range from $15 to $40 per person, depending on the duration and inclusions.

Exploring Ronda's Iconic Landmarks

Ronda is home to a wealth of iconic landmarks that bear witness to its illustrious past and cultural heritage. From towering bridges to ancient fortresses, each landmark tells a unique story of Ronda's evolution through the ages.

1. Puente Nuevo: The Majestic Bridge of Ronda

Standing as a symbol of Ronda's engineering prowess and architectural splendor, the Puente Nuevo spans the breathtaking depths of the El Tajo gorge, connecting the old and new quarters of the city. Marvel at the panoramic views of the surrounding countryside from the bridge's lofty vantage points, and witness the mesmerizing spectacle of the Guadalevín River as it winds its way through the rugged landscape below.

Entrance to the Puente Nuevo is free, and visitors can

access the bridge at any time of day. For the boat experience, consider visiting during sunrise or sunset when the soft golden light bathes the landscape in a warm glow, casting shadows that dance upon the ancient stone walls.

2. La Ciudad: Ronda's Old Town

Lose yourself in the timeless charm of Ronda's Old Town, where centuriesold monuments and architectural wonders await around every corner. Wander through the labyrinthine streets of the Albaicín quarter, where the echoes of Moorish influence linger in the air. Discover hidden gems such as the Plaza de España, a tranquil oasis adorned with lush gardens and ornate fountains.

The Old Town of Ronda is open to visitors throughout the day, with no admission fees required. Take your time to explore its narrow alleys and hidden squares, and don't be afraid to get lost in its labyrinthine charm.

3. Casa del Rey Moro: Tracing Moorish Influence

Journey back in time to the era of Moorish rule as you explore the Casa del Rey Moro, a historic mansion nestled on the cliffs overlooking the El Tajo gorge. Delve into the fascinating history of Ronda's Moorish past as you wander through the labyrinthine gardens and subterranean tunnels that once served as secret escape routes during times of siege.

Admission to the Casa del Rey Moro is priced at $8 per person and includes access to the gardens, tunnels, and panoramic viewpoints. Guided tours are available for an additional fee and offer deeper insights into the mansion's history and architecture.

Sampling Ronda's Gastronomic Delights

No visit to Ronda would be complete without indulging in its culinary delights, where every dish tells a story of tradition, flavor, and passion. From rustic taverns to upscale restaurants, Ronda offers a myriad of gastronomic experiences that tantalize the taste buds and nourish the soul.

1. Culinary Gems of Ronda

Embark on a gastronomic journey through Ronda's culinary landscape, where the freshest ingredients and timehonored recipes come together to create culinary masterpieces. Sample traditional Andalusian fare such as gazpacho, salmorejo, and pescaíto frito, washed down with a glass of locally produced wine or sherry.

Prices for dining experiences in Ronda vary depending

on the establishment and menu selection. Expect to pay an average of $20 to $50 per person for a meal at a midrange restaurant, while upscale dining experiences may cost upwards of $100 per person.

2. Traditional Tapas Tour: Indulging in Andalusian Flavors

Embark on a culinary adventure through Ronda's bustling tapas bars and taverns, where the art of tapas comes to life in a symphony of flavors and textures. From savory jamón ibérico to succulent albondigas, each bite offers a tantalizing glimpse into Andalusia's rich culinary heritage.

Join a guided tapas tour to uncover the hidden gems of Ronda's culinary scene, led by local experts who know the best kept secrets of the city's gastronomic treasures. Prices for tapas tours typically range from $30 to $80 per person, including food and drink tastings at multiple establishments.

Indulge your senses and savor every moment as you navigate Ronda's charming streets, explore its iconic landmarks, and sample its gastronomic delights. Let the spirit of Andalusia guide your journey, and immerse yourself in the timeless allure of this enchanting city where every experience is a celebration of life and culture.

Chapter 2

Immersing in Ronda's Culture

A Journey of Discovery

In the heart of Andalusia, Ronda pulsates with a cultural vibrancy that transcends time and captivates the soul. From the haunting melodies of flamenco to the colorful tapestry of festivals and the architectural splendor of its museums, Ronda invites travelers to immerse themselves in its rich cultural heritage and vibrant traditions.

Flamenco: The Heartbeat of Ronda

Step into the intimate world of flamenco, where passion, emotion, and rhythm converge to create an electrifying spectacle that resonates with the soul. In Ronda, flamenco isn't just a performance—it's a way of life, an expression of the city's deepest emotions and traditions.

To experience the essence of flamenco in Ronda, venture into the heart of the city's historic quarter, where intimate tablaos and flamenco venues await. One such venue is Tablao Flamenco El Quinqué, nestled amidst the winding streets of Ronda's Old Town. Here, under the soft glow of candlelight, passionate dancers, soulful singers, and virtuoso guitarists come together to weave a mesmerizing tapestry of sound and movement.

Tickets to flamenco performances at venues like Tablao Flamenco El Quinqué typically range from $20 to $50 per person, depending on the seating arrangement and performance schedule. For the most authentic experience, opt for a small, intimate venue where you can feel the heat of the dancers' footsteps and the raw emotion in their voices.

Flamenco performances in Ronda usually take place in

the evening, with shows starting around 8:00 PM and lasting until the early hours of the morning. Arrive early to secure a good seat and immerse yourself fully in the passion and intensity of this timeless art form.

Festivals and Celebrations: Embracing Ronda's Vibrant Spirit

Throughout the year, Ronda comes alive with a kaleidoscope of festivals and celebrations that celebrate its cultural heritage and traditions. From the exhilarating atmosphere of the Feria de Pedro Romero to the solemnity of Semana Santa, each festival offers a unique glimpse into the soul of Ronda.

1. Feria de Pedro Romero: Revelry in Ronda's Bullfighting Tradition

Held annually in September, the Feria de Pedro Romero pays homage to Ronda's deeprooted connection to bullfighting, a tradition that has endured for centuries. The festival takes its name from Pedro Romero, a legendary matador who hailed from Ronda and achieved fame and acclaim in the bullfighting arena.

During the Feria de Pedro Romero, the streets of Ronda come alive with vibrant parades, traditional music, and exhilarating bullfights that capture the essence of Andalusian culture. Locals and visitors alike don traditional attire and gather in the city's plazas to dance, sing, and revel in the festive atmosphere.

Admission to the Feria de Pedro Romero is free, with various events and activities taking place throughout the weeklong celebration. For an authentic experience, immerse yourself in the festivities by joining in the dances, sampling traditional cuisine, and cheering on the brave matadors as they face off against fierce bulls in the ring.

2. Semana Santa: Ronda's Seminal Holy Week Celebrations

Semana Santa, or Holy Week, holds a special place in the hearts of Ronda's residents, who come together to commemorate the solemn rituals and traditions of the Catholic faith. From solemn processions to elaborate religious ceremonies, Semana Santa offers a profound and deeply moving experience for both participants and observers alike.

In Ronda, Semana Santa unfolds with a sense of reverence and devotion, as intricate floats adorned with religious icons wind their way through the city's streets, accompanied by somber music and the rhythmic sound of marching bands. Witness the pageantry and piety of Semana Santa by lining the procession route or joining the faithful as they gather in churches and squares to pay homage to their faith.

Semana Santa in Ronda typically takes place in the week leading up to Easter Sunday, with various events and processions held throughout the city. Check local listings and event schedules for specific dates and times, and be sure to arrive early to secure a prime viewing spot along the procession route.

Art and Architecture

Ronda's artistic and architectural heritage is a testament to the city's enduring legacy as a center of creativity and innovation. From the meticulously preserved artifacts of the Museo Lara to the breathtaking beauty of the Palacio de Mondragón, Ronda's cultural treasures invite travelers to embark on a journey through time and imagination.

1. Museo Lara: A Journey through Ronda's Past

Housed within a meticulously restored 18thcentury mansion, the Museo Lara offers a captivating glimpse into Ronda's storied past and cultural heritage. Explore its diverse collections of artifacts, antiques, and archaeological finds, which span millennia of history and encompass a wide range of themes and subjects.

From ancient Roman artifacts to medieval weaponry and Moorish ceramics, the Museo Lara offers a comprehensive overview of Ronda's cultural evolution and historical significance. Delve into the mysteries of the past as you wander through its labyrinthine halls and galleries, guided by informative exhibits and interactive displays.

Admission to the Museo Lara is priced at $8 per person, with discounted rates available for students, seniors, and children. The museum is open daily from 10:00 AM to

7:00 PM, offering ample opportunities to explore its treasures at your leisure.

2. Palacio de Mondragón: Witnessing Architectural Grandeur

Perched atop the cliffs overlooking the El Tajo gorge, the Palacio de Mondragón stands as a majestic testament to Ronda's architectural splendor and Moorish heritage. Built during the Moorish era and later expanded during the Renaissance, the palace showcases a harmonious blend of Islamic and Christian design elements, reflecting the cultural diversity and artistic ingenuity of its creators.

Step into the opulent interiors of the Palacio de Mondragón and marvel at its exquisite courtyards, ornate archways, and intricately carved ceilings. Explore its richly furnished rooms and galleries, which house an impressive collection of decorative arts, ceramics, and textiles spanning centuries of history.

Admission to the Palacio de Mondragón is priced at $10 per person, with guided tours available for an additional fee. The palace is open Tuesday to Sunday from 10:00 AM to 5:00 PM, offering visitors ample time to immerse themselves in its architectural grandeur and historical significance.

As you delve into Ronda's cultural tapestry, let the rhythms of flamenco, the pageantry of festivals, and the beauty of its art and architecture captivate your senses and ignite your imagination. Embrace the spirit of discovery and embark on a journey of cultural exploration that will leave an indelible mark on your heart and soul.

Chapter 3

Outdoor Nature Escapes in Ronda

As the sun bathes the rugged landscapes of Andalusia in golden hues, Ronda beckons adventurers to explore its pristine wilderness and breathtaking vistas. From invigorating hikes along scenic trails to exhilarating explorations of the surrounding countryside, Ronda offers outdoor escapes that immerse travelers in the raw beauty of nature.

Hiking the Trails

Step off the beaten path and into the embrace of nature as you embark on a journey along Ronda's scenic hiking trails. From verdant forests to rugged mountainscapes, each trail offers a unique opportunity to connect with the land and discover hidden treasures along the way.

One of Ronda's most iconic hiking trails is the Camino de los Molinos, which winds its way through the picturesque countryside, past ancient windmills and cascading waterfalls. This moderatelevel trail offers hikers a chance to immerse themselves in the region's natural beauty while enjoying panoramic views of the surrounding landscape.

For a more challenging adventure, consider tackling the Sendero de los Alcornocales, a rugged trail that meanders through dense cork oak forests and rocky terrain. Along the way, hikers may encounter diverse wildlife, including wild boar, deer, and a myriad of bird species.

To make the most of your hiking experience in Ronda, be sure to pack plenty of water, snacks, and sun protection, as temperatures can soar during the midday hours. Wear sturdy hiking shoes with good traction to navigate uneven terrain safely, and always adhere to trail markers and signage to avoid getting lost.

Additionally, consider joining a guided hiking tour led by experienced local guides, who can provide invaluable insights into the region's flora, fauna, and geological features. Guided hiking tours in Ronda typically range from $30 to $80 per person, depending on the duration and difficulty level.

Exploring the Surrounding Countryside

Venture beyond the city limits of Ronda and into the surrounding countryside, where a world of adventure awaits. From quaint villages to rolling vineyards, the countryside offers a diverse array of experiences that showcase the natural beauty and cultural heritage of the region.

Embark on a scenic drive along the Ruta de los Pueblos Blancos, or White Villages Route, which winds its way through charming hilltop villages adorned with whitewashed facades and narrow cobblestone streets. Stop in picturesque towns such as Zahara de la Sierra and Grazalema, where time seems to stand still amidst the timeless beauty of the Andalusian countryside.

For those seeking a taste of Andalusian hospitality, consider visiting one of the region's renowned wineries for a guided tour and tasting experience. Bodegas La Sangre de Ronda, located just a short drive from the city center, offers visitors an opportunity to sample a variety of locally produced wines while learning about the winemaking process.

To enhance your exploration of the surrounding countryside, consider renting a car or joining a guided day trip that includes transportation and visits to key attractions. Day trips from Ronda typically range from $50 to $150 per person, depending on the itinerary and inclusions.

Tajo de Ronda: Admiring Nature's Sculpture

Perched high atop the precipitous cliffs of the El Tajo gorge, the Tajo de Ronda stands as a breathtaking testament to the raw power and beauty of nature. Carved over millennia by the rushing waters of the Guadalevín River, this natural wonder offers visitors a mesmerizing panorama of sheer rock faces, verdant valleys, and azure skies.

To fully appreciate the splendor of the Tajo de Ronda, venture to its most iconic vantage points, such as the Mirador de Aldehuela and the Puente Nuevo. From these elevated viewpoints, travelers can admire the sheer magnitude of the gorge and the ancient city perched precariously on its rim.

For the ultimate adventure, consider embarking on a guided rock climbing or abseiling excursion, where experienced guides will lead you on an adrenaline fueled journey down the vertical cliffs of the gorge. These exhilarating experiences offer a unique perspective of the Tajo de Ronda and provide an unforgettable opportunity to connect with nature in a thrilling new way.

The Tajo de Ronda is accessible year round, with no admission fees required for visiting its viewpoints. For the best experience, plan your visit during the early morning or late afternoon hours, when the soft light of dawn or dusk bathes the landscape in a warm golden glow.

As you explore Ronda's outdoor escapes, allow yourself to be swept away by the awe inspiring beauty of nature and the boundless spirit of adventure that awaits around every corner. Whether hiking along scenic trails, exploring the surrounding countryside, or admiring the majestic Tajo de Ronda, let the natural wonders of Andalusia ignite your senses and nourish your soul.

Address: Ronda, Malaga Province, Andalusia, Spain

Contact Information: For guided tours and outdoor activities, contact Ronda Tourism Office: +34 952 18 71 19

Amenities: Some hiking trails may have restroom facilities and picnic areas along the route. Guided tours may include transportation, snacks, and equipment rental.

Website: (https://www.turismoderonda.es/en/)

Chapter 4

Ronda's Hidden Gems

Unveiling Treasures beyond Expectations

In the heart of Andalusia, Ronda conceals its secrets within its labyrinthine streets, awaiting the curious traveler eager to uncover its hidden gems. Amidst the whitewashed walls and cobblestone paths lie treasures that whisper tales of history, nature, and culture, inviting exploration beyond the obvious.

Secret Gardens and Scenic Views

Amidst the urban tapestry of Ronda lies the Alameda del Tajo, a verdant sanctuary perched on the edge of the El Tajo gorge. Here, beneath the shade of ancient trees, one can pause to admire the breathtaking panorama stretching across the rugged landscape. Opening its gates at sunrise and bidding farewell at sunset, the Alameda del Tajo offers solace and serenity to those seeking respite from the city's bustle.

Venture further into the city's heart to discover the Palacio de los Mondragones, where Renaissance gardens beckon with their timeless allure. For a modest fee of $12, visitors can wander amidst sculpted hedges, fragrant blooms, and whispering fountains, lost in the tranquility of this hidden oasis.

To uncover Ronda's secret gardens and scenic views, embrace spontaneity and wander without agenda through its maze of streets. Let curiosity be your guide, and you may stumble upon courtyards adorned with bougainvillea, or viewpoints offering vistas that steal your breath away.

Off the Beaten Path: The Thrill of Discovery

Away from the clamor of tourist crowds lie the Baños Arabes, silent witnesses to Ronda's Moorish past. Venture into their cool depths for a glimpse into history, where vaulted ceilings and ornate tiles whisper tales of bygone eras. Guided tours, priced at a modest $6, reveal the secrets of these ancient baths, inviting travelers to immerse themselves in Ronda's rich cultural tapestry.

In the heart of the city, the Mercado de Abastos pulsates with the rhythm of local life, offering a feast for the senses. Amidst the vibrant chaos, sample the flavors of Andalusia, savoring the essence of jamón ibérico and the tang of ripe olives. Lose yourself amidst the colors and aromas, and discover the soul of Ronda in its bustling market hall.

To uncover Ronda's hidden treasures, embrace spontaneity and follow the path less traveled. Strike up conversations with locals, who hold the keys to the city's secrets, and allow curiosity to lead you to unexpected discoveries.

Wine Tasting in Ronda: A Toast to Tradition

No journey through Ronda is complete without indulging in its liquid gold—its wine. Amidst sundrenched hills and rolling vineyards, Ronda's wineries beckon with promises of sensory delights.

At Bodega Descalzos Viejos, housed within a historic monastery, visitors embark on a journey through time and taste. Guided tours, priced at $20, lead guests through vineyards and cellars, culminating in a tasting of Ronda's finest wines paired with local delicacies.

For a more intimate experience, venture to Bodega Joaquin Fernandez, where the winemaker shares his passion for viticulture with visitors. Guided tastings, priced at $15, offer a glimpse into the heart and soul of Ronda's winemaking tradition.

To savor Ronda's liquid treasures, linger over each sip, allowing flavors to dance upon your palate. Engage with winemakers, who pour their passion into every bottle, and let the spirit of Ronda infuse each glass with its essence.

As you delve into Ronda's hidden gems, embrace the thrill of discovery and allow the city's secrets to unveil themselves before you. In every hidden garden, forgotten alleyway, and cherished bottle of wine, discover the essence of Ronda—the soul of Andalusia, waiting to be discovered.

Chapter 5

Practical Tips for Travelers

In the enchanting city of Ronda, practical knowledge is the key to unlocking its hidden treasures and embracing its vibrant culture. From navigating transportation to selecting the perfect accommodation and mastering essential phrases, these practical tips ensure a seamless and memorable journey through the heart of Andalusia.

Getting Around Ronda: Transportation Tips and Tricks

Navigating the picturesque streets of Ronda is a breeze with a variety of transportation options catering to every traveler's needs.

1. Public Transportation: Ronda boasts a reliable network of buses connecting key attractions and neighborhoods within the city. The local bus service operates from early morning until late evening, with tickets priced at an average of $1.50 per ride. For the utmost convenience, consider purchasing a rechargeable travel card, available at select outlets and offering discounted fares for frequent travelers.

2. Walking: With its compact size and pedestrian friendly layout, Ronda is best explored on foot. Lace up your walking shoes and wander through its historic streets, taking in the sights and sounds of this captivating city at your own pace. Don't forget to wear comfortable footwear, as some areas may feature cobblestone streets and uneven terrain.

3. Taxi Services: For those seeking a more personalized travel experience, taxi services are readily available throughout Ronda. Taxis can be hailed on the street or booked in advance through reputable companies, with fares starting at around $5 for short distances within the city center. Be sure to confirm the fare with the driver before starting your journey, and always carry small denominations of cash for payment.

To make the most of your transportation experience in Ronda, plan your itinerary in advance and familiarize yourself with the city's bus routes and schedules. Opt for walking whenever possible to immerse yourself fully in Ronda's charm, and consider using taxis for longer distances or late night journeys.

Accommodation Options for Every Budget

From luxurious boutique hotels to cozy guesthouses and budget friendly hostels, Ronda offers a diverse range of accommodation options to suit every traveler's taste and budget.

1. Boutique Hotels: For those seeking a touch of

elegance and sophistication, Ronda's boutique hotels beckon with their stylish interiors and personalized service. Stay at Hotel Montelirio, nestled in the heart of the Old Town, where spacious rooms overlook the iconic Puente Nuevo. With rates starting at $150 per night, Hotel Montelirio offers a luxurious retreat amidst Ronda's historic charm.

2. Guesthouses: Embrace the warmth of Andalusian hospitality at one of Ronda's charming guesthouses, where personalized service and cozy accommodations await. Casa Duende del Tajo, located steps away from the Tajo de Ronda, offers comfortable rooms and stunning views of the gorge below. Prices for guesthouses in Ronda typically range from $50 to $100 per night, depending on the season and amenities.

3. Hostels: Travelers on a budget will find plenty of affordable accommodation options in Ronda's hostels, where communal spaces and vibrant atmospheres foster a sense of camaraderie among guests. Stay at Albergue Ronda, located within walking distance of the city center, where dormitory style rooms and shared facilities provide budget conscious travelers with a comfortable place to rest. Hostel rates in Ronda start at around $20 per night, making them ideal for backpackers and solo travelers.

To ensure a memorable stay in Ronda, research accommodation options in advance and book early, especially during peak travel seasons. Consider factors such as location, amenities, and guest reviews when selecting your accommodation, and don't hesitate to reach out to hotel staff or hosts with any special requests or inquiries.

Essential Phrases and Local Etiquette

Mastering a few key phrases in Spanish and understanding local customs and etiquette can enhance your travel experience in Ronda and foster meaningful connections with locals.

1. Greetings and Courtesy: Start your interactions with a warm greeting, such as "Buenos días" (Good morning), "Buenas tardes" (Good afternoon), or "Buenas noches" (Good evening). Show respect by using "Por favor" (Please) and "Gracias" (Thank you) in your conversations, and remember to address people with "Señor" (Sir) or "Señora" (Madam) as a sign of courtesy.

2. Dining Etiquette: When dining out in Ronda, it's customary to wait to be seated by the host or hostess. Keep in mind that mealtimes in Spain tend to be later than in other countries, with lunch typically served between 1:30 PM and 3:30 PM, and dinner starting around 8:30 PM or later. Embrace the local custom of sharing dishes and taking your time to enjoy each course, and don't forget to leave a small tip of 510% for exceptional service.

3. Navigating Transportation: When using public transportation or taxis in Ronda, always greet the driver with a friendly "Hola" (Hello) or "Buenos días" (Good morning) before stating your destination. Pay attention to local customs, such as offering your seat to elderly passengers or pregnant women on buses, and always respect designated waiting areas and queues.

To immerse yourself fully in Ronda's culture and community, take the time to learn basic Spanish phrases and observe local customs and etiquette. Embrace each interaction as an opportunity to connect with the people of Ronda and gain insights into their way of life.

As you embark on your journey through Ronda, let these practical tips be your guide, empowering you to navigate the city with confidence and embrace its rich tapestry of history, culture, and hospitality.

Chapter 6

Beyond Ronda: Day Trips and Excursions

In the heart of Andalusia, Ronda serves as a gateway to a world of enchanting landscapes, rich cultural heritage, and breathtaking coastal vistas. Embark on unforgettable day trips and excursions from Ronda, each offering a unique glimpse into the diverse tapestry of the region.

A. Exploring the Pueblos Blancos: A Journey through Andalusia's White Villages

Nestled amidst the rolling hills and rugged terrain of Andalusia, the Pueblos Blancos, or White Villages, beckon travelers with their timeless charm and picturesque beauty. Embark on a journey through these iconic villages, each adorned with whitewashed facades and winding cobblestone streets.

Start your exploration with a visit to Zahara de la Sierra, perched atop a hill overlooking a shimmering reservoir. Wander through its narrow alleys and medieval fortress, soaking in panoramic views of the surrounding countryside. Admission to the castle costs approximately $5, and it is open daily from 10:00 AM to 6:00 PM.

Continue your journey to Grazalema, renowned for its stunning natural scenery and artisanal craftsmanship. Explore the village's artisan workshops, where skilled craftsmen produce traditional woolen blankets and shawls. Don't miss the opportunity to sample local delicacies, such as payoyo cheese and homemade pastries, at one of Grazalema's charming cafes.

For a taste of Andalusian history, venture to Arcos de la Frontera, perched dramatically atop a sandstone ridge overlooking the Guadalete River. Wander through its labyrinthine streets and historic churches, marveling at the Moorish architecture and medieval fortifications. Entrance to the Castillo de los Arcos costs approximately $4, and it is open daily from 10:00 AM to 6:00 PM.

To make the most of your journey through the Pueblos Blancos, consider joining a guided tour that provides insights into the history, culture, and traditions of each village. Guided tours typically range from $50 to $100 per person and may include transportation, entrance fees, and lunch.

Coastal Escapes

Escape the inland heat and venture to Ronda's nearby seaside retreats, where sundrenched beaches, azure waters, and coastal charm await.

Journey to the picturesque town of Marbella, renowned for its luxurious resorts, golden beaches, and vibrant waterfront promenade. Spend the day soaking up the sun on Marbella's renowned beaches, such as Playa de la Fontanilla or Playa del Cable, where pristine sands and clear waters beckon swimmers and sunbathers alike.

For a taste of luxury, indulge in a beachfront meal at one of Marbella's chic restaurants or beach clubs, where fresh seafood and Mediterranean flavors take center stage. Prices for beachfront dining in Marbella typically range from $20 to $50 per person, depending on the restaurant and menu selection.

Alternatively, venture to the charming coastal town of Estepona, where cobbled streets, flower filled plazas, and historic landmarks beckon visitors to explore its rich heritage. Stroll along the Paseo Marítimo, Estepona's scenic seaside promenade, lined with palm trees and vibrant flowers, or explore the town's historic Old

Town, home to charming cafes, boutique shops, and colorful murals.

To enhance your coastal escape from Ronda, consider renting a car for the day to explore the coastal towns at your own pace. Alternatively, join a guided day trip that includes transportation and visits to key attractions along the coast. Day trips to Marbella or Estepona typically range from $50 to $100 per person, depending on the itinerary and inclusions.

Day Trips to Nearby Cultural Gems

Discover the rich tapestry of Andalusia's history and culture with day trips to nearby historic enclaves, where ancient ruins, medieval castles, and architectural wonders await.

Begin your journey with a visit to the ancient city of Antequera, renowned for its rich archaeological heritage and stunning monuments. Explore the UNESCO World Heritagelisted Dolmens of Antequera, a collection of megalithic burial mounds dating back over 5,000 years. Admission to the Dolmens costs approximately $5, and they are open daily from 10:00 AM to 6:00 PM.

Continue your exploration with a visit to the historic town of Ronda la Vieja, the original site of Ronda before it was relocated to its current location. Explore the ruins of the Roman city, including its ancient baths, amphitheater, and necropolis, which offer glimpses into the daily life and culture of ancient Andalusia. Admission to Ronda la Vieja is free, and it is open to visitors during daylight hours.

For a glimpse into medieval Spain, venture to the hilltop town of Carmona, where narrow streets, fortified walls, and historic landmarks tell tales of centuries past. Explore the town's Moorish fortress, stroll through its charming plazas, and admire its historic churches and palaces. Entrance fees to Carmona's historic sites vary, with most attractions open daily from 10:00 AM to 6:00 PM.

To maximize your day trips to nearby cultural gems, plan your itinerary in advance and prioritize key attractions based on your interests and preferences. Consider joining guided tours or hiring local guides to provide insights into the history, architecture, and culture of each destination.

As you venture beyond Ronda's borders, immerse yourself in the diverse landscapes and rich cultural heritage that define Andalusia, creating memories that will last a lifetime.

Chapter 7

Ronda: A Photographer's Paradise

In the heart of Andalusia, Ronda stands as a timeless canvas, beckoning photographers from around the globe to capture its essence through the lens. From ancient bridges spanning dramatic gorges to winding streets steeped in history, Ronda offers a wealth of photographic opportunities waiting to be explored.

Capturing Ronda's Essence Through the Lens

To truly capture the soul of Ronda, photographers must immerse themselves in its rich tapestry of sights, sounds, and textures. Each corner of the city holds a story waiting to be told, a moment waiting to be frozen in time.

Begin your photographic journey at the iconic Puente Nuevo, Ronda's most famous landmark and a testament to human ingenuity and architectural prowess. As the golden light of dawn bathes the gorge in hues of amber and rose, capture the bridge's timeless silhouette against the backdrop of the rugged landscape below. Experiment with different angles and perspectives to convey the bridge's grandeur and majesty, from wideangle shots that encompass the entire structure to closeups that reveal intricate details of its construction.

Venture into Ronda's historic Old Town, where narrow cobblestone streets and whitewashed buildings whisper tales of centuries past. Lose yourself amidst the labyrinthine alleyways, where every turn reveals hidden courtyards, ornate doorways, and sundappled plazas. Embrace the play of light and shadow, capturing the interplay of textures and colors that define Ronda's architectural charm.

For a glimpse into Ronda's Moorish heritage, explore the winding alleys of the La Ciudad neighborhood, where ancient walls and crumbling arches bear witness to centuries of history. Frame the intricate tilework and decorative motifs that adorn the facades of centuriesold buildings, capturing the essence of Andalusia's rich cultural heritage.

As the day draws to a close, ascend to the Mirador de Aldehuela, where panoramic views of the city await. From this vantage point, watch as the sun dips below the horizon, casting a warm glow over Ronda's rooftops and valleys. Capture the fleeting moments of twilight, when the sky is ablaze with hues of orange and crimson, and the city below is bathed in a soft, ethereal light.

To truly capture Ronda's essence through the lens, embrace spontaneity and serendipity, allowing the city to reveal its hidden treasures and moments of beauty. Keep your camera close at hand, ready to capture the magic of each fleeting moment, and allow your intuition and creativity to guide your photographic journey.

Photography Tips and Spots

In Ronda, every corner presents a photographic opportunity waiting to be discovered. Whether you're a seasoned professional or an amateur enthusiast, these photography tips and spots will help you capture the beauty of Ronda with precision and artistry.

1. Golden Hour Magic: Make the most of Ronda's golden hours—the period shortly after sunrise and before sunset—when the soft, diffused light bathes the city in a warm, golden glow. Head to the Puente Nuevo or Mirador de Aldehuela during these magical moments to capture the city's iconic landmarks aglow with the hues of dawn or dusk.

2. Exploring the Old Town: Lose yourself amidst the

labyrinthine streets of Ronda's Old Town, where every corner holds a photographic gem waiting to be unearthed. Explore hidden alleys, charming courtyards, and sundrenched plazas, and keep your camera ready to capture the intricate details and textures that define Ronda's architectural charm.

3. Chasing Shadows and Reflections: Embrace the interplay of light and shadow that defines Ronda's urban landscape, capturing the dramatic contrasts and silhouettes that unfold throughout the day. Seek out reflections in tranquil fountains, shimmering windows, and ancient cobblestones, adding depth and dimension to your compositions.

4. Venturing off the Beaten Path: Don't hesitate to venture off the beaten path and explore lesser known corners of Ronda, where authenticity and character abound. Wander through the La Ciudad neighborhood, where Moorish influences mingle with Spanish architecture, or explore the tranquil gardens and hidden courtyards that lie tucked away amidst the city's winding streets.

5. Elevated Perspectives: Ascend to Ronda's panoramic viewpoints, such as the Mirador de Aldehuela or the Parador de Ronda, for bird's eye views of the city and its breathtaking surroundings. Experiment with different vantage points and perspectives, capturing sweeping vistas and dramatic landscapes that showcase Ronda's natural beauty.

To make the most of your photographic journey in Ronda, embrace curiosity and experimentation, allowing the city to inspire and guide your creative vision. Keep your senses attuned to the nuances of light, texture, and atmosphere, and allow yourself to be swept away by the timeless charm and beauty of this enchanting Andalusian gem.

Conclusion: Farewell to Ronda

As your journey through the winding streets and storied landscapes of Ronda draws to a close, take a moment to reflect on the timeless allure of this enchanting Andalusian gem. From ancient bridges spanning dramatic gorges to whitewashed villages perched atop sunkissed hills, Ronda leaves an indelible mark on the soul of every traveler who ventures within its embrace.

Reflecting on Ronda's Timeless Allure

In the heart of Andalusia, Ronda stands as a testament to the enduring spirit of Spain—a land steeped in history, culture, and tradition. As you bid farewell to its cobblestone streets and sun dappled plazas, take with you the memories of moments shared beneath the shadow of the Puente Nuevo, the laughter of children echoing through the Alameda del Tajo, and the whispers of history that linger in every stone.

Reflect on the echoes of centuries past that resonate through Ronda's ancient walls and Moorish arches, bearing witness to the triumphs and tribulations of generations gone by. Embrace the timeless allure of its landscapes, from the rugged cliffs of the Tajo de Ronda to the rolling vineyards of the surrounding countryside, each telling a story of resilience, beauty, and grace.

As you journey beyond Ronda's borders, carry with you the lessons learned and the connections forged amidst its vibrant tapestry of sights, sounds, and flavors. Let the spirit of Ronda guide your footsteps as you venture forth into the world, a beacon of inspiration and discovery lighting the path ahead.

Inspiring Memories and Future Adventures

As you bid farewell to Ronda, let your heart be filled with the promise of future adventures and the memories of moments shared in its embrace. Let the beauty of its landscapes and the warmth of its people linger in your thoughts, inspiring you to seek out new horizons and embrace the wonders that await.

Take with you the lessons learned from Ronda's rich tapestry of history and culture, carrying them as talismans of wisdom and insight on your journey through life. Let the friendships forged and the connections made be a testament to the power of travel to unite hearts and minds across borders and boundaries.

And as you embark on new adventures and explore distant lands, know that Ronda will always be waiting, its doors open wide to welcome you back with open arms. For in the heart of every traveler who has wandered its streets and breathed its air, Ronda remains forever etched—a timeless beacon of beauty, wonder, and possibility.

Farewell, dear traveler, to Ronda—the jewel of Andalusia, the cradle of history, and the keeper of dreams. May your memories be as enduring as its ancient walls, and may your adventures be as boundless as the horizons that stretch before you.

As you bid farewell to Ronda, carry its spirit with you always, and let its timeless allure inspire your journeys near and far. Until we meet again, may the memories of Ronda continue to enrich and illuminate your path?

Printed in Great Britain
by Amazon

41011258R00046